Yahi Archery

Saxton T. Pope

Printing Statement:

Due to the very old age and scarcity of this book,
many of the pages may be hard to read due to the
blurring of the original text, possible missing pages,
missing text, dark backgrounds and other issues
beyond our control.

Because this is such an important and rare work, we
believe it is best to reproduce this book regardless of
its original condition.

Thank you for your understanding.

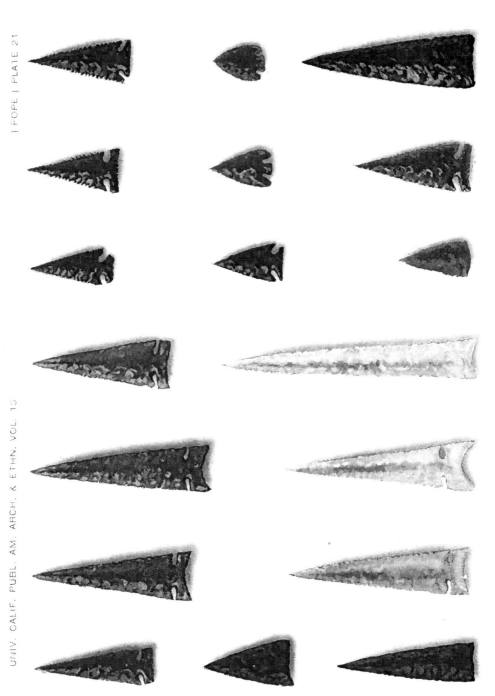

ARROWHEADS OF OBSIDIAN, FLINT, AND GLASS, MADE BY ISHI

UNIVERSITY OF CALIFORNIA PUBLICATIONS

IN

AMERICAN ARCHAEOLOGY AND ETHNOLOGY

Vol. 13, No. 3, pp. 103-152, plates 21-37   March 6, 1918

YAHI ARCHERY

BY

SAXTON T. POPE

CONTENTS

INTRODUCTION

Archery is nearly a lost art. Among civilized peoples it survives only as a game. It is well known, however, that even as late as two centuries ago the bow was a vigorous competitor with the flintlock in warfare. Benjamin Franklin at the beginning of the Revolution seriously considered the possibility of arming the American troops with the longbow, as a cheaper and more effective weapon than the flintlock[1] musket. That the archery even of the American Indian was, during the early periods of occupation, substantially as effective as the musketry of the period is attested in the historic records of some of the explorers.[2] Such aboriginal archery has, of course, undergone a great decadence since the rifle has supplanted the bow. It is now

[1] See letter from Benjamin Franklin to Major-General Lee, in Memoirs of the late Charles Lee, second in command in the service of the United States of America of America during the revolution. . . London, 1792, p. 240.

[2] See, for example, the narrative of Cabeza de Vaca concerning the Indians of Florida, in Buckingham Smith, Relation of Alvar Nuñez Cabeza de Vaca, New York, 1871, p. 30.

almost extinct. As a matter of fact, we have very little accurate information as to how the Indians used their weapons, and still less as to how they made them. The present paper is an attempt to present the facts concerning the archery of one tribe, the Yahi or Deer Creek Indians of north central California, the most southerly division of the Yanan[3] stock, as represented in the person of its last survivor, Ishi, who lived from 1911 to 1916 at the University of California. The paper will deal first with the very interesting methods of the Yahi for the manufacture of the implements of archery, and second, their style of shooting.

It must be remembered that the performances of civilized archers, who practice with the bow as a sport, far surpass those of savages. It is a curious fact that archery was brought to perfection only after the bow became obsolete as a serious weapon. It is interesting, therefore, to compare the Yahi "style" with that of the more skilful archers who follow the rules of the modern game.

Ishi, the native informant for the present paper, comes of a tribe famous for its fighting qualities. The group lived to a considerable extent on wild game, and the bow was their glory and their delight. We have no reason to believe that their skill or the strength of their weapons was inferior to that of the average American savage. Concerning the informant himself, the following might be said:

Ishi loved his bow as he loved nothing else in his possession.

He knew what a gun was, but he had never shot one until after 1911 when he entered civilization. The bow he had used ever since boyhood. When captured he had no weapons, though a bow and many arrows were taken from his lodge by those who first discovered the camp where the remnant of his people were living. Some of these arrows we later recovered, some through the generosity of the finders and some by purchase, but his original bow is missing.

What the writer knows of Ishi's archery is based upon three years' association with him. In this period many hours were spent in making bows and arrows, in talking about shooting, in target practice, and in hunting trips in the fields and woods. During the years 1913 and 1914 there was opportunity for two extended trips in the mountains in his company. Dr. J. V. Cooke and the present writer took up the practice of archery in 1912 under Ishi's guidance, at first according to the Indian's own methods, though later we followed the English style. At first Ishi was our master in marksmanship, but at

[3] Edward Sapir has published Yana Myths in volume 9 of the present series.

the end of a few months we were able to outdo him at target work, and to equal his performances in shooting game. This does not in any way imply greater skill on our part, but does point clearly to the actual superiority of the "civilized" methods.

In speaking of the techniques of manufacture used by Ishi, it must be remembered that he soon adopted civilized tools in this work. The jackknife and file supplanted the obsidian blade and the scraper of sandstone. He only returned to his primitive ways when requested to show the processes he formerly performed.

He was a most painstaking and finished workman. His dexterity and ingenuity were delightful to watch. No better specimens of arrowheads, shafts, and bows are contained in the Museum of the University than those made by him. Probably better ones were never made anywhere. His eye for form and symmetry was perfect.

TECHNICAL TERMS

A bow has the following parts: A back, that part away from the archer; a belly, the concave side, when full drawn; a handle or hand grip, a portion near the center for holding the weapon; limbs, that part between the handle and the extremities. These extremities usually have notches, or some contrivance to maintain the string in position, called nocks. The process of bending a bow and attaching the string to the ends is called bracing it. The amount of pull on the string, necessary to draw an arrow a proper distance before discharging it from the bow, may be ascertained in pounds by means of a scale or balance. This is called the "weight" of the bow.

THE BOW

Ishi called the bow *man'i*. He made bows of many woods while under observation, but upon an expedition into his country three years after his capture he showed us the tree from which the best bows were made. It was the mountain juniper. He made a stave from one of these trees on the spot, though it was later ruined.

He described another tree from which his tribe made bows, apparently the incense cedar. This, he said, was chopped down by the one man in his tribe who owned an iron axe, and split with wedges of deer horn into proper-sized staves. To obtain the wood for his bow he broke a limb from the tree, which seems to have been the custom before the days of axes.

The Indian with the axe seems to have been the bow maker of the vicinity. He also owned a long knife, and was known as *Chunoyahi*, that is, Atsugewi or Hat Creek Indian. Of his prowess with the bow, Ishi told us many tales.

Juniper wood Ishi called *nogu'i*. Yew wood he did not seem to have used, though he knew of it and said that other tribes used it. His name for this was *hulogos'i*. He knew that its leaves were poisonous to eat.

While with us he used eucalyptus, tanbark oak, red cedar (*tiyun'i*), hickory, ash, juniper, and yew for his bows. All of these were of the same general shape and size, and all were backed with sinew. Yew, of course, produced the best weapon. His standard of measurement for a good bow was to hold a stave diagonally across his chest with one end in his right hand at the hip, and the left arm extended straight out at an angle of 45 degrees from the horizontal. The distance between these points was the proper length for a bow. This measured in his own case four feet and two inches. The width of the bow at the middle of each limb was three or four fingers, according to whether a light hunting bow or a powerful war bow was wanted.

The shape of his bow was a short, flat stave, with limbs wider at their center than at the handle, sometimes recurved at their outer extremity, tapering gracefully to small short nocks at the ends.

His wood, after being split or partially blocked out from a limb, was laid in a horizontal position in a warm, sheltered place. Here it seasoned. But as to what time of year to cut it, or how long to season it, Ishi seemed to have no set opinions.

The process of shaping the bow was that of scraping with flint or obsidian. With infinite patience and care he reduced the wood to the proper dimensions. In the finishing work he used sandstone. The measurements of two of his best bows are as follows:

Number 1–19590. Length, 44 inches. Diameters, at handle, ⅝ by 1½ inches; at midlimb, 9/16 by 1⅛ inches; at nock, 5/16 by ¾ inches. Pulls 40 pounds.

Bow in possession of author. Shown in use in plate 31. Length, 54½ inches. Diameters, at handle, ¾ by 1⅝; at midlimb, ½ by 1¾; at nock, ¼ by ½ inches. Pulls 45 pounds.

He seemed to have had no great respect, as the English do, for the white sap wood of yew or cedar. Although he placed this at the back of his bow, he did not hesitate to cut through its grain to attain a symmetrical form, and just as often he would scrape most of it away, leaving only a thin stratum of white at each edge. At the handle a cross section of the bow was oval, while a section through the mid-limb was much flatter.

In some of his bows the last six inches of the limbs were recurved. This was accomplished by holding the back of the bow, at this point, on a hot rock while pressure was applied at the ends, bending the wood over the stone, shifting the bow back and forth, until the requisite curve had been obtained. Then, while the wood cooled, Ishi held it pressed against his knee, which was protected by a pad of buckskin.

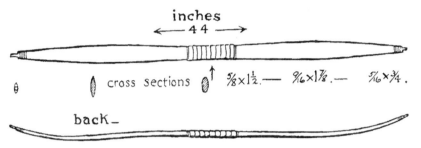

Ishi's short bow

After the bow was shaped and finished smoothly on the belly, the sinew was applied to the back, which had been left rather rough. As backing for his bow, Ishi used either the dorsal fascia obtained from a deer, or he teased out the long tendons, *bama*, from the hind legs. These strips were from eight to fourteen inches long, and when dry were about the thickness of parchment.

Preparatory to using this tissue he soaked it in warm water for several hours. The back of his bow, the side having the sap wood on it, he smeared thickly with glue. In his native state he made this glue, so he said, by boiling the skin of salmon and macerating it while hot. While with us he was very enthusiastic over our common liquid glue and disdained the use of hot furniture glue. He permitted this coating of glue to dry. Now, having his sinew wet, he chewed these strips until they were soft and pulpy and then carefully laid them in parallel lines down the back, overlapping the ends as he went. This process required a great deal of tissue and much patience. Having applied the sinew, he bound it on with ribbons of maple bark running spirally about the bow. This he removed after the expiration of "one sleep." As the sinew dried, it contracted and tended to draw the ends of the bow into a reversed position. After this had happened, he applied more glue to the surface. Several days later, when all the backing was thoroughly dry and hard, he filed and scraped it very smooth, filing the overlapping margins level with the edges of his bow.

Strips of sinew during the process of "backing" were folded over the nocks of the bow. He now served or wrapped the ends of the bow with strips of tendon, covering the nock proper and running about an inch down the limb. Here he let his work rest for days or weeks, exposing it to the sunlight and permitting the wood to season fully. During this waiting period he made the bow string or *chalman'i*. The tendons used in this were of a finer quality than those used before and were obtained from the outer, more slender group of tendons in the deer's shank. These he stripped far up into their origin in the muscle bundles, tearing them free with his teeth.

If fresh, he simply chewed this tissue and teased it apart into threads no larger than floss silk. If dry, he soaked it in warm water before chewing it. He then proceeded to spin a string by fixing one end of a bundle of tendon strips to a stationary point and rolling the other end between his fingers in a single strand. As he progressed down the string he added more threads of tendon to the cord, making a very tight, simple twist one-eighth of an inch thick. When about five feet long, he twisted and secured the proximal end, leaving his twisted cord taut between two points. The last smoothing-up stage he accomplished by applying saliva and rubbing up and down its length. The finished bow string was now permitted to dry. Its final diameter was about three thirty-seconds of an inch. After it was dry he formed a loop at one end by folding back some three inches of string, tapering it by scraping, and serving two of the three inches securely with more tendon. He seemed to have no idea of splicing, nor did he know any clever knots. Moreover, he never used glue at this point. In fact this loop was the weakest part of his string and not infrequently came apart, when, in disgust, he would tie a single loop knot and forego the finished effect of the unknotted self loop. Nor had he any idea of serving his string with any binding at the nocking point, where the arrow rests.

At this stage, Ishi was ready to string the bow. He designated the end of the stave which grew uppermost in the tree as the *chunna*. "face," and over the nock in this end he slipped the loop of his string. To fail to shoot with this end uppermost, he said, would cause the arrow to miss its mark.

In stringing the bow for the first time, he seated himself, placing the upper nock behind his left heel, the belly toward him, the handle against his right knee, the lower limb upward in his left hand. In this position he bent the bow and fastened the string about the other nock. His method of securing the string was as follows: he wound it twice aroung the nock, passed under the bowstring, turned backward and wound in the opposite direction several laps, then fixed the end by a couple of slip knots. Usually he made his string with a tapering extremity which rendered it easier to fasten. Then he cautiously drew his bow and observed its bend. On cold days, Ishi warmed his bow over a fire before attempting to brace it. The ideal bow, to his mind, curved in a perfect arch at all points, and at full draw represented a crescent. The center bent with the limbs and was the bow's weakest point. A forty-five inch bow he drew twenty-five inches. No yew wood could stand such an arc without backing. In fact he broke two bow-staves, testing them at my request, prior to the application of sinew.

Where the contour showed the bow too strong, he filed or scraped it on the belly side, thus gradually distributing the bend evenly along the bow. About the middle he bound a ribbon of buckskin, making a hand grip some five or six inches wide. This buckskin thong was about half an inch wide and ran spirally about the bow, not over-lapping, fastened at each end by an extra wrapping of string or sinew.

Ishi showed no tendency to anoint his weapon with grease, nor to apply any protective coat, though later he learned the value of shellac in preserving his backing from dampness. The great aversion he had to shooting while any fog or moisture was in the air rather indicates that his bow was without the coverings of fat, wax, or resin so frequently used by archers in other parts of the world.

Usually Ishi made no effort to decorate his bow, though he spoke of painting it, and led me to infer that this was done only after the implement had shown some peculiar virtue, or had figured in some deed of valor. The one bow he embellished while with us he marked with three green transverse stripes just above the handle and below the nocks, and three long snaky lines running down the back. He said that red also was an appropriate color.

When finished and seasoned, these bows pulled, or "weighed," when drawn to twenty-five inches, between thirty-five and fifty pounds. His favorite hunting bow weighed forty pounds.

When not in use he kept his bows in a leather quiver, or wrapped in a cloth. The tail of a mountain lion was considered an admirable cover for a bow. The bow was always laid in a horizontal position. To stand a bow upright, according to his theories, was to keep it working; if left standing it would "sweat" and become weak. If a child touched a bow, it brought bad luck. Nor should a child step over it while it lay on the ground, for this would cause it to shoot crookedly. If a woman touched Ishi's bow, it was a serious contamination. The bow must be washed and cleaned with sand. He was most careful not to keep his bow strung too long but furnished the loop with a bit of cord, which extended from nock to loop, and served to keep the bow string from getting out of place while the bow was unbraced. After unstringing he often gave his bow a slight bend backward to restore its straightness; this is considered very bad practice by English archers.

A good bow was one whose string made a high musical note when tapped with an arrow or snapped with the fingers. It should sing the note "tin, tin, tin." This was the "chief's bow." One whose note was dead and unmusical, Ishi treated with contempt.

By placing the upper end of his braced bow at the corner of his open mouth and gently tapping the string midway between the end and center he caused clear musical notes to be produced. This sounded like our jew's-harp, and by altering the shape of the buccal cavity he was able to create a series of tones sufficient to form a melody relating to a story of wonderful deeds with the bow. He sang of a great archer who dipped his arrow point in the sea, then in the fire, drew a mighty bow, and shot at the sun. His arrow flew like the north wind, and entering the door of the sun, put out its light. Then all the world became dark, men shivered with cold, and from this time they grew feathers on their bodies to make them warm.

THE ARROW

The arrow was called *sawa*.

Of all the specimens of arrows in the University Museum, scarcely any show such perfect workmanship as those of Ishi. His proportions and finish are of very high order.

At the time of the rediscovery of the remnant of the tribe, a number of arrows were secured from the huts, which doubtless represent his average work. Later, while with us, he made scores of arrows of various shapes and sizes. Apparently some arrows, those of great length, measuring a yard, and having large heads, were purely for ornamental purposes, or intended to be given as presents, or possibly to be used in time of war. His hunting shafts were of two kinds—obsidian pointed, and blunt. For shooting small game, such as birds and rabbits, the latter were used. For killing deer, bear, and predaory animals, sharp arrows were used. Here, if the object shot at were missed, a broken arrow-point resulted. The arrow shafts were made of several kinds of wood. Those obtained from his hut in Tehama County seem to be of hazel, *humoha*, and this was a favorite wood with him. A native bamboo-like reed was also a great favorite. Dogwood and mountain mahogany he also used. Other shaft woods pointed out by him were *bakanyau'an* (*Philadelphus Lewisii*), *sawa'i* ("arrow bush," *Paeonia Brownii*), and *loko* and *habaigili'i*, unidentified. Later, as the result of a modification of ideas he underwent in our company, he adopted the commercial $\frac{5}{16}$-inch birch dowel as the ideal material, probably because of its accessibility.

In the case of cane arrows, a wooden "foreshaft," six to eight inches long, was invariably added, and such foreshafts were sometimes added to wooden arrows. They were of hazel, buckeye (*bahsi*), wild currant (*wahsu'i*), and perhaps other woods. The foreshaft was normally heavier material than the main shaft.

In general it may be said that his typical hunting arrow was a hazel stick, with a foreshaft, the entire length being 29 inches. The diameter at the middle was $\frac{11}{32}$ inch; and the total weight was 330 grains. The feathering of the arrow consisted of three plumes from a buzzard's wing, $4\frac{3}{4}$ inches long, $\frac{3}{8}$ inch wide. They were trimmed straight to the forward end, where their width was about $\frac{1}{8}$ inch, and terminated $\frac{3}{4}$ inch from the nock of the arrow. At each end the feathers were bound down with sinew.

In gathering wood for arrows he generally selected the tall, straight shoots of hazel where it grew in competition with other shrubs or trees, cutting them about a yard long, their greatest diameter being little more than three-eighths of an inch. These he stripped of bark with his thumb nail. He always made arrows in groups of five. Thus he would select the best of his sticks, and collecting them in groups, bind them together securely with a cord. In this bundle they were permitted to season, lying in a horizontal position. After any period from a week to a year these sticks might be used.

The first process in manufacture was that of straightening his shafts. To do this he either made a small heap of glowing embers from a fire or utilized a hot stone. He applied pressure with his thumbs on the convex side of any irregularity or bend in a shaft, and holding this near the heat, passed the wood back and forth before the stone or coals. When the wood was warm, it gave very readily to pressure. In less than a minute any curve or crook could be straightened out. The wood after cooling always retained its new position. Glancing down the axis of his shaft from time to time, Ishi gauged its straigl ness. To burn or discolor the wood was evidence of bad techniqu Smoothing was accomplished by scraping and rubbing the arr shaft between two pieces of sandstone. He sometimes finished t shaft by rolling it back and forth on the thigh with his right pal while he worked it with a piece of sandstone held in his left hand. I this means he could "turn" a shaft almost as accurately as if a lat were used.

Where a foreshaft was to be added, the length of the main sha was 21 inches. At the smaller end he cut a notch for the bow stri with a bit of obsidian, making this nock $\frac{5}{32}$ of an inch wide and 3 inch deep. In larger arrows he deepened this to $\frac{1}{2}$ inch. The oth end of the shaft was next drilled out to accommodate the foreshaft.

His method of drilling was as follows: Placing a sharp piece bone, point up, in the ground, and steadying it with his toes, he rotat the shaft perpendicularly upon this point. The motion here was ide tical with that employed in making fire by means of a drill and ba stick, the stick being rolled between the palms with downward pres ure. The excavation averaged an inch in depth and a quarter of inch in diameter, and ran to a point. During this drilling process t lower end of the shaft was tightly bound with sinew or cedar co to keep it from splitting. One end of the foreshaft was formed in a spindle and made to fit this socket, leaving a slight shoulder whe the two segments met. Salmon glue or resin was used to secure unio and the joint was bound with macerated tendon for the distance of inch or more.

When a group of five arrows had been brought to this stage completion, he painted them. His favorite colors were green and re At first he insisted that these were the only colors to use, since th had the effect of making the arrows fly straight. After we began excel him in marksmanship he scraped all his arrows and painte them red and blue, perhaps to change his luck. The shafts obtain from his hut were of these latter colors, but at least the blue American pigment, perhaps secured during nocturnal prowlings vacant cabins.

Red, he told me, came from the earth and was made with fir Blue he obtained from a plant "like a potato"; green from a pla "like an onion"; black from the eye of salmon or trout.[4] The pi

---

[4] Ishi designated *Lathyrus sulphurea, kununutspi'i,* as yielding a yellow pai for arrows. The "onion" from which green was obtained may have been a pla related to the lily *Fritillaria lanceolata,* which he called *t'aka,* although he declar this species to produce a salmon-colored dye. *Commandra umbellata, punentsau* in his language, was also used for painting arrows.

ments were mixed with the gum or sap of some trees. He had no opportunity to explain the process more fully. When with us he used the ground pigments of commerce, with which he mixed an alcoholic solution of shellac.

The University Museum has a sample of red pigment obtained from the Yahi Indians before Ishi's capture, and it is the usual red ochre.

The design employed in painting usually consisted of alternating rings of red and blue a quarter of an inch wide, with a wide space between two groups of the stripes, sometimes occupied by red or blue dots, or snaky lines running lengthwise. Only that space which was later to be spanned by the feathers was painted. The design was usually three rings near the nock, then ten rings at the smaller end of the feather.

In applying his paint he used a little stick of wood, or drew a small bunch of bristles, set in resin, through a quill, making a brush. To make the rings of color he clamped the arrow shaft between his left arm and chest, while he rotated it with the left hand. In his right, which was steadied on his knee, he held the brush with its coloring matter. In making serpentine lines he used a little pattern of wood or deer-hide, cut with a zigzag edge, along which he passed his brush. These figures seemed to have no symbolic meaning to him. Apparently they were simply standard designs.

When the paint was dry, he ran a broad ring of glue above and below it, at the site of the subsequent binding which holds the feathers. This he let dry.

Many kinds of feathers were used by Ishi on his arrows—eagle, hawk, owl, buzzard, wild goose, heron, quail, pigeon, flicker, turkey, bluejay. He preferred eagle feathers but admitted that they were very hard to get. While with us he used either the tail or pinion feathers from the domestic turkey. Like the best archers he put three feathers from the same wing on each arrow.

The first process of preparing the feather was to separate its laminae at the tip and split the shaft down its length by pulling it apart. Only the strip forming the posterior part of the original quill was used. He placed one end of this strip on a rock, clamping his great toe firmly upon it, and pulled it taut with the left hand, while with a sharp knife he shaved the upper surface of the aftershaft or rib to the thinness of paper. By scraping with an obsidian chip he now reduced it to translucent thinness, leaving no pith on it. Feathers so scraped are very flexible but the laminae tend to stand at an angle of

thirty degrees from the perpendicular when set on the arrow. Ha
ing finished many feathers this way he collected them in groups
three, according to their similarity of form and color, and bound ea
group with a short bit of thread. When ready to apply them to t
arrow, these sets of three, each set from the same wing, were soak
in warm water. When soft, the feathers were shaken dry, separate
and each tested for its strength by pulling its two extremities. The
gathering about half an inch of laminae with the tip of the aftersha
and holding this end securely, he ruffled the rest of the laminae bac
ward, in order to have a clear space over which to apply sinew
the next stage. Each feather in turn was thus made ready.

Very delicate deer tendons, having been split and soaked in wate
were now chewed to a stringy pulp and drawn from the mouth in th
ribbons about a foot long. One end he held by the teeth, the oth
was attached to the arrow by a couple of turns near the nock. I
then placed each feather in succession in its position; one perpe
dicular to the nock, two at its opposite edges, making equidista
spaces between them. As he rotated the shaft, the tendon being he
in his teeth, he bound the rib and a half inch of laminae togeth
down to the shaft, smoothing all with his thumb nail at the last. T
reversed position of the rest of the laminae at this point made his wo
easy. Having treated one arrow, he let it dry while he fixed each
the remaining four.

The next step was to draw the anterior extremity of the featheri
down into position. Beginning at the last painted ring where the gl
commenced, he stripped off the laminae in preparation for the app
cation of tendons. Again he spun out a ribbon of tissue, and setti
each feather in place, holding the top one with his left thumb, and t
other two with the first and second fingers respectively, he began bin
ing with the sinew. After proceeding a few turns, he released l
hold and straightened each feather to its final position, which w
about one-sixteenth of an inch off the direct line down the arrow, ve
ing off slightly toward the concave side of the feather. Now, drawi
the feathers tight and snug, he cut the rib about half an inch lo
and completed the binding by rotation, plus a final smoothing with l
thumb nail. In applying the tendon, he was careful to make a clo
spiral, never overlapping his sinew except at the last few turns. Ea
arrow, being thus feathered, was put in the sunshine to dry. After
number of hours he would pick up a shaft and by beating it gent
against his palm, restore the laminae to their natural direction, fluffi

ut the feathering. After having stroked the thoroughly dry feathers
o settle them, he trimmed them by laying them on a flat piece of
wood, using a straight stick as a ruler and running a sharp chip of
obsidian along this edge. Obsidian flakes are quite as sharp as a good
razor, and cut feathers better.

His feather usually had a straight edge, and had a height of ⅛
inch at the forward end and ¾ or ½ inch at the nock end. Sometimes
they were cut in a slightly concave line, and usually no trimming was
done near the nock, but the natural curve of the feather tip was left
here, making a graceful finish to his work.

Instead of standing perpendicularly to the shaft, as has been
recommended by our ancient English archers, Ishi's feathers were set
at an angle to his arrow and tended to fall or lie closer to the shaft
after much use or being carried in the quiver. This position does
seem to have the advantage, however, of giving a better spin to the
arrows in flight, which, of course, tends toward greater accuracy.
Some of Ishi's feathers were not more than three inches long, and
those on his exhibition or war arrows were the full length of a hawk's
pinions—almost a foot.

In none of his arrows which were made in the wilds was there any
evidence of glue between the feather and arrow shaft; but while with
us he occasionally ran a little glue beneath his feather after binding
it on.

In his native state, he seems to have used no protective over the
sinew to keep out moisture—not even fat—nor did he apply any finish
or varnish to the surface of his shafts.

The arrow in the condition just described was now accurately cut
to a certain length. His method of measurement was to hold the butt
against his own sternal notch and then, reaching along the shaft with
his left hand, almost in his shooting position (as described below), he
cut the shaft off at the end of his left forefinger. This gave a length
of about twenty-nine inches. The cutting of the shaft was done with
a filing motion of an obsidian knife. Later he used a bit of broken
hack-saw. The point of the shaft was then slightly rounded, and if
intended for small game, bound with sinew. If obsidian points were
to be used, a notch similar to that intended for the bow string was
made, and so cut that when the arrow was drawn on the bow, this
notch was in a perpendicular position. The idea in placing the head
in a vertical plane was that in this position it entered between the
ribs of an animal more readily.

Ishi did not seem to know that in flight an arrow revolves qui
rapidly and necessarily must shift from its plane immediately up
leaving the bow. With the old English archers, the broad-head w
placed in the same plane with the nock, for the same mistaken reaso
With the English, of course, the bow is held almost perpendicula
while with most Indians, as with Ishi, the bow has a more or le
horizontal position in shooting.

ARROW POINTS[5]

For making arrowheads, bone and obsidian and flint were used l
the Yahi. Flint Ishi designated as *pana k'aina* and seemed to like
because of its varied colors. But *hahka* or obsidian was in common
use, and among the Yahi it served even as money. Boulders of ob
dian were traded from tribe to tribe throughout his country. Th
probably came by way of the Hat Creek Indians from Shasta Coun
and other districts where this volcanic glass was prevalent.

A boulder of obsidian was shattered by throwing another rock
it. The chunks thus obtained were broken into smaller size by hol
ing a short segment of deer horn or piece of bone against a projecti
surface, and smartly striking it a glancing blow with a stone. T
resulting flakes of obsidian best suited for arrowheads were rough
three inches long, an inch and a half wide and half an inch thic
Selecting one of these, according to its shape and grain, he began t
flaking process.

Protecting the palm of his left hand by means of a piece of bue
skin, and resting the left elbow on the left knee, he held the obsidia
tightly against the palm by folding his fingers over it. The flak
was a piece of deer horn bound to a stick about a foot long. Holdi
this instrument securely in his right hand, the stick resting benea
the forearm for leverage, he pressed the point of the horn against t
obsidian edge with vigor, and fractured or flaked off a small bit. I
reversing the position of the obsidian in his hand and attacking t
opposite edge with the flaking tool, repeating in a painstaking w
this manœuver after several flakings, he slowly fashioned his arr
point, making long deep chips or light finishing flakes, as the cond
tion required. He used deer horn for the heavier work, but whi
with us he chiefly employed a soft iron rod three-sixteenths of an in
in diameter and eight inches long, having a handle or padding of clo

---

[5] Compare the article by N. C. Nelson, Flint Working by Ishi, *in* the Holm
Anniversary Volume, Washington, 1916, pp. 397–401.

ound about it for a distance of six inches. The tool must be a sub-
tance that will dent slightly and thus engage the sharp edge of
obsidian. Tempered steel utterly fails to serve this purpose. His
flaking tools were shaped something like a screw driver, only rounded
instead of square at the point. These he filed quite sharp. When the
obsidian had assumed the desired triangular shape, he exchanged his
buckskin pad for a sort of thumb-piece of the same material. Holding the arrow point firmly on this with the left index finger, he selected
a small flaking tool about the side of a shoemaker's awl, made of a
wire nail driven into a wooden handle, and fashioned the notches near
the base of the arrowhead by pressing the point of the flaking tool
against the ball of the thumb.

To make a head of this type required about half an hour. He
made them in all sizes and shapes. Large spike-like heads were for
gift arrows and war. Medium size heads, perhaps $1\frac{1}{2}$ inches long,
$\frac{1}{4}$ inch wide, and $\frac{1}{4}$ inch thick, were for ordinary deer shooting, while
small, flat oval heads were for shooting bear.

Apparently it was Yahi custom to do most of the making of bows
and arrows away from the camp, in secluded spots particularly favorable to this employment. At least this was true of the making of
arrowheads; partially so, no doubt, because of the danger entailed,
and partially because it was strictly a man's job.

Ishi said that the men congregated in a circle, in a warm sunny
place, painted their faces with black mud to keep the flying flakes
out of their eyes, and maintained silence—either for ceremonial purposes or to avoid getting pieces of flint or glass in the mouth. Among
their theories of disease, the one which they most usually invoked was
the supposed presence of bits of obsidian or spines of cactus and
similar sharp objects in the system. The medicine man gave support
to this theory, moreover, by the "magical" extraction of such objects
from his patients, by means of sucking the painful spot.

If by chance a bit of glass flew in the eye while flaking arrowheads,
Ishi would pull down his lower eyelid with the left forefinger, being
careful not to blink or rub the lid. Then he bent over, looking at the
ground, and gave himself a tremendous thump on the crown of the
head with the right hand. This was supposed to dislodge the foreign
body from the eye.

After much close work he frequently suffered from eyestrain head-
ache. His distant vision was excellent, but like many Indians he was
astigmatic. He also complained of fatigue and cramp in his hands
after prolonged flaking.

The arrowheads were first set in the shaft by heating pine resi
and applying it to the notched end, then moulding it about the ba
of the obsidian point. When firm, the point was further secured l
binding it with sinew, back and forth, about the tangs and arour
the shaft. Three wraps were made about each notch, and the tend(
was wound about the arrow for the distance of half an inch imm
diately below the arrowhead. After drying, this secured the he;
very firmly and was quite smooth. A little polishing with sandsto
gave a fine finish to the bin ling.

These heads frequently were képt in a little bag of skin, and n
attached to the arrow till a few hours before the expected hunt. Ext
heads were kept in readiness to substitute for those broken durii
use. Large oval blades were bound on short handles and used
knives. Still larger blades of the same type, on a long handle, we
used as spears.

After some experience in shooting at targets, Ishi devised a su
stitute for the regular target arrow pile, or head. He made blu
points from thin brass tubing or steel umbrella sticks, cut into o
inch lengths. He filed these with deep transverse notches across o
end and pounded this portion into a blunt conical shape. These hea
he set on his shafts with glue.

THE QUIVER

When upon a prolonged hunt, Ishi carried as many as sixty arro
with him, though his quiver seldom contained more than a score. T
extra arrows he kept covered with a skin and bound with bucksk
thongs, and he carried them slung over his shoulder.

His quiver, now in the University Museum, was made from t
skin of an otter, the fur side out, and the hair running upward.
measures 34 inches in length, 8 inches in width at the upper end, a
4 inches at the lower. The skin had been removed whole, save for ;
incision over the buttocks. The hind legs had been split and l(
dangling, while the fore legs were two sheaths of skin inverted with
the quiver. The mouth was sewn with tendon, and the split tail serv(
as a carrying strap. Four punctures in the animal's back show(
where the toggles of a salmon spear had entered and had had ex
indicating its method of capture. A strip of buckskin was also stitch(
to the outlet of the quiver, and, running inside, was again stitch(
two-thirds of the way down. Its use seems to have been as a carryir
strap.

Besides his arrows he carried his bow in the quiver, and slung
ll over the left shoulder. It was not easy to extract arrows from the
uiver quickly, so it was customary to carry a few in the hand. These,
during the act of shooting, Ishi either laid on the ground or held
beneath his right arm. Owing to his peculiar method of shooting, this
did not interfere when he drew his bow.

HANDLING OF THE BOW

His system of shooting was as follows: Taking his bow from the
uiver, he placed the lower end on his partially flexed left thigh.
While he held the bow by the center with the left hand—its back was
down—his right hand caught the string between forefinger and thumb.
The other fingers held the upper end near the nock. Now, depressing
he handle and bending the bow, he slipped the loop of the string over
he nock. If, perchance, the string were too long, he unstrung the

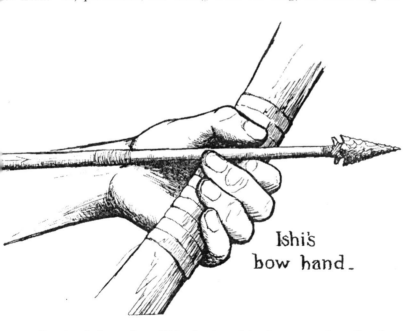

Ishi's
bow hand—

ow and twisted the string till it shortened to the proper length, when
he again bent and braced his bow. When strung, the distance between
he string and the hand grip was about four and a half inches. He
hen would place four or five arrows beneath his right arm, points to
he front, leaving one in the hand. Holding the bow diagonally across
he body, the upper end to the left, he "nocked" his arrow by lay-

ing it on the right side of the bow. It crossed the middle of the b(
where the first and second fingers of the left hand received it and he
it from slipping; it was also a little distance away from the bow. Th
refinement of technique was necessary to avoid rubbing the feather
which were longer than the space between the bow and the strin
The bow itself he clamped in the notch between the thumb and finge
of the left hand. He did not grip it tightly, even when full draw
It poised in this notch, and even when the arrow was released it w
only retained from springing from the hand by a light touch of l
fingers. Some Indians, he said, had a little strap on the handle
prevent the bow jumping out of the hand.

The arrow, when full drawn, rested on the bow, steadied in positi(
by the slight touch of his thumb on one side, the middle finger tip
the other. When the arrow left the string, at the moment of relea:
the bow revolved, or turned over completely, in his hand, so that t
back of the bow was toward him.

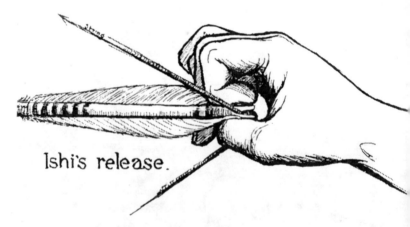

Ishi's release.

The arrow release (the letting fly of the arrow) was a modificati(
of that known as the Mongolian type. That is, he "drew" the b(
with the right thumb flexed beneath the string. On the thumb na
he laid the end of the middle finger, to strengthen the hold. T
index finger, completely flexed, rested on the arrow to keep it fr(
slipping from the string. The extremities of the feathers, being ne
the nock, were neatly folded along the shaft in the grip of th(
fingers, to prevent them from being ruffled.

Ishi knew of several releases, saying that certain other tribes us
them. The primary type, that where the arrow butt is gripped betwe
the thumb and the flexed forefinger, he said certain Indians use
and it seemed to be a criterion of strength.

There are five known types of arrow release or methods of holding the arrow on the string while the bow is drawn. These were determined and named by E. S. Morse.[6]

The Primary release is that most naturally used by the novice. It draws the arrow by pinching it between his thumb and flexed forefinger. This is not a strong grip on the arrow, though practice undoubtedly strengthens the hold. No robust archery, according to English standards, has ever been done with this release. Yet it is the only one reported from many primitive peoples, perhaps even the method most commonly followed by uncivilized tribes.

The Secondary release is similar, but the middle finger assists in the pull by pressing on the string.

The Tertiary release holds the arrow between the thumb and straightened forefinger. It may also place other fingers on the string to assist in the pull.

The Mongolian or Asiatic release is chiefly used with the composite bow, and consists of pulling the string with the flexed thumb, more or less supported by the other fingers, while the arrow is merely steadied in position by contact with the forefinger, and by being held in the angle between the thumb and forefinger. This method reaches full effectiveness when a sharp-edged thumb ring is worn to engage the string.

The Mediterranean release was known to the ancients and is that used in English archery and by the Eskimo. The first three fingers, unassisted by the thumb, draw the string, while the engaged arrow rests between the first and second fingers.

Ishi's release is of peculiar interest because its precise type has never been described before; also because the fundamental method of which it is a variety, the Mongolian, has until now not been reported in America.

A series of tests of the comparative strength of these various arrow releases, made by the writer with a spring scale attached to an arrow and cord, yields the following average pulls:

Primary, 25 pounds.
Primary, with an arrow having a grip or notch in the end to assist the draw, 35 pounds.
Secondary, 40 pounds.
Tertiary, 60 pounds.
Mongolian, 45 pounds.
Mongolian, with a Japanese-type shooting glove to protect the thumb, 55 pounds.
Mediterranean, 80 pounds.

---

[6] Bulletin of the Essex Institute, Salem, XVII, 145–198, 1885.

Greater experience may have somewhat favored the result for t Mediterranean method, but there is no doubt that it is the most powe ful of all known releases.

As Ishi drew with the back of his hand uppermost, he extended l bowarm horizontally and kept it straight, midway between a later and forward position. His right hand he drew till its back ca beneath his chin, the end of his radius touching the top of his sternu Thus he looked straight along his arrow with both eyes open. In th position his eyes were considerably above the nock of the arrow a he therefore had to allow for over-shooting his mark.

He changed the position of his drawing hand for different rang For near shots, his right hand was often drawn as high as his mout His extreme length of draw was not over twenty-six inches, while f small game and near shots he shortened this to eighteen or twen inches. He never drew any shaft to the head. In drawing, his rig arm was held close to the body, while the shoulder was marked elevated. This gave him a hunched appearance, but it permitted h to hold arrows under his arm, and in other ways must have favor his peculiar mode of shooting. It also threw his right arm and for arm into the same plane with his bow.

Before making any careful shot it was his invariable habit glance down his arrow and straighten with his fingers any slig curvature that might be present.

Nocking, drawing, aiming, and releasing, all were done with three seconds. He dwelt on his aim about a second, and shot entire by intuition, not by point of aim. For long shots he attempted to ass the flight of his arrow by quickly pushing forward his bow arm he shot.

A point blank range is that condition in aiming where the tip the arrow seems to rest on the object to be hit. With him this was abo fifty yards, and at over sixty yards his bow hand obscured his vision, that he first aimed, then further elevated his bow hand before releasir With the English method of shooting, where the arrow lies at the le of the bow, the hand does not interfere with the vision, unless in she of more than a hundred yards, because the left eye can see past t hand.

After discharge of his arrow, Ishi maintained his shooting positi for a second, as good archers always do. He preferred to shoot kne ing or squatting; this seems to have been the best posture for ga shooting. In kneeling, he usually placed his right knee on the grour

Shooting with us, especially at targets, he stood facing the target, or turning his left side slightly toward it. His position was rather insecure, knees flexed a trifle, feet about four inches apart. His body he held quite erect, though in stalking game he shot from a crouching position.

He never used a wrist guard or "bracer" on his left arm to protect it from the string, although he nearly always pulled up his shirt sleeve. This was to avoid striking any clothing with the string, which would check the flight of the arrow. At times the string did strike his forearm, and bruise it, and after prolonged shooting his left wrist was often sore and ecchymosed. Leather protection for his forefinger he sometimes used in target shooting, but neither the glove nor bracer seemed needed for the intermittent shooting during a hunt.

In nocking his arrow, he paid no particular attention to the cock feather, or that opposite the nock. It rested against the bow as often as away from it. With nearly all modern archers, this is considered very bad technique. Since most of the feathers were soft, this however did not seem much to disturb the flight of the arrow.

ISHI'S RECORDS WITH THE BOW

There are no records of aboriginal archery with which to compare those of civilized times. That the American Indian was a good shot is conceded by all who know him, and fiction makes him out an incomparable archer, capable of deeds outrivaling those of William Tell and the redoubtable Robin of Sherwood Forest. But no authentic scores exist. It is therefore a privilege to have been able to compare the shooting of an unspoiled American Indian with that of modern archers.

So far as target shooting is concerned, it is well known that the greatest archer of all times was Horace Ford of England, whose records of 1857 were not approached by any in history, and have not been surpassed since.

There are two well recognized rounds in archery. The English or York round consists in shooting six dozen arrows at one hundred yards, four dozen at eighty yards, and two dozen at sixty yards, and adding the score thus attained. The American round consists in shooting thirty arrows at each of the distances, sixty, fifty, and forty yards. The target used is a circular straw mat four feet in diameter, four inches thick, covered with a facing on which are five concentric rings. The central ring or gold is nine and one-half inches in diameter, while each circle is one-half this in width.   Their values are 9, 7, 5, 3, points.

Because of the great distance, and his inability to hit the targ often enough to warrant compiling a score, Ishi seldom shot the Yo round.   But we have many records of his scores at the Americ round.   It must be conceded that an archer may be a poor target sh and yet at the same time be a practical and accurate archer in huntin Ishi's best scores at the American round are as follows, 30 arrows bei shot at each distance:

October 23, 1914.
    60 yards, 10 hits,   32 score
    50 yards, 20 hits,   92 score, 2 golds
    40 yards, 19 hits,   99 score, 2 golds

    Total..........49 hits, 223 score 4 golds

May 30, 1915.
    60 yards, 13 hits,   51 score
    50 yards, 17 hits,   59 score
    40 yards, 23 hits,   95 score, 1 gold

    Total..........53 hits, 205 score, 1 gold

The best score for the American round is at present held by E. Rendtorff, and is thus recorded:

    60 yards, 30 hits, 208 score
    50 yards, 30 hits, 226 score
    40 yards, 30 hits, 234 score

    Total..........90 hits, 668 score

A good score will total 90 hits, 500 score.   My own best round is hits, 538 score.

At ten and twenty yards Ishi was proportionately much m accurate, and while not consistent, he could hit objects three or f inches in diameter with such frequency that it was a commonpl event.   Out of every five arrows, one or two surely would reach t mark.   In his native state, his targets were small bundles of str about the size of a rabbit or quail, or he shot at a small hoop in moti

At shooting on the wing or at running game, he did not seem be correspondingly adept.   At so-called turtle shooting, or shooti up in the air and having the arrow strike the object in descent, he w not proficient.   In rapid shooting he could just discharge his th arrow while two were in the air; unlike the alleged performance Hiawatha, he could not keep ten shafts aloft at once.   Catlin repo that the Mandans could keep eight arrows in the air at one time.

Ishi's greatest flight shot was 185 yards. No doubt had he prepared himself for distance shooting he could have surpassed this; but using his 40-pound hunting bow and the lightest arrow in his quiver, this was his extreme length. After Ishi's death, I shot his bow, with an especially light arrow with a closely cropped feather, a distance of 200 yards. The greatest modern shot was that done by Ingo Simon, at La Toquet, France, in 1914, of 459 yards, with a very old Turkish composite bow. The greatest recorded flight shot with the English long bow was made by John Rawlins in 1794, a distance of 360 yards. The best American flight shot is 290 yards, done by L. W. Maxson, in 1891. Shooting a six-foot yew bow weighing 75 pounds with a flight arrow, my own best shot is 275 yards.

To ascertain the casting power of what Ishi considered an ideal bow, I had him select one that he considered the best, from the entire number in the Museum. This was a Yurok bow of yew heavily backed with sinew and corresponded closely in proportions to those of his own make. After warming it carefully and bracing it, Ishi shot a number of light flight arrows. His greatest cast was only 175 yards. Its weight was less than 40 pounds.

Besides the fact that Ishi, in common with all savages, failed to understand the optics and ballistics of archery, his arrows were of such unequal weight and dissimilar shape and size, that it is not surprising that his marksmanship was erratic. A difference of ten grains in the weight of a shaft, or a slight difference in the height of the feathers, will cause an arrow shot sixty yards to fly several feet higher or lower than its predecessor.

The length of time required for Ishi's hunting shafts to fly 100 yards was 4 seconds. The angle of trajection was 30 degrees. The weight of these arrows was 1 ounce; their power of penetration was sufficient to pierce our target, which consisted of a piece of oil cloth, 2 gunny sacks, and 4 inches of straw target, entirely traversing these bodies. A steel hunting point, shot from 40 yards, readily penetrated an inch into pine. On striking a tree, the entire point and an inch of the shaft were often buried in the trunk.

The angle of elevation necessary for his arrow to fly one hundred yards is much greater than that needed for our target arrows. Shooting a 48-pound bow with a five-shilling, or one-ounce arrow, my elevation is 15 degrees, while under the same conditions with a 65-pound bow it is as low as 10 degrees. The time required for a 100-yard flight of this latter is $2\frac{2}{5}$ seconds. The average velocity of an arrow is reckoned at 120 feet a second.

HUNTING

At a very early period in our association with the Yahi, we under took various little hunting excursions, and upon two occasions wen upon extended trips into the mountains.

In shooting small game, such as quail, squirrels, and rabbits, Ishi was very proficient. His method was that of still hunting; walking over the ground very quiet and alert, always paying particular atten tion to wind, noise, and cover. He was indefatigable in the persistence with which he stalked game, and seldom left a clump of brush in which he knew or suspected the presence of game, until all means of getting it had been tried.

His vision was particularly well trained, and invariably he sighted the game first. This acumen was manifest also in the finding of arrows Ishi nearly always could find a shaft in the grass or brush where we overlooked it.

He shot rabbits as close as five yards. On the other hand I have seen him shoot a squirrel through the head at forty yards. The usual killing distance was between ten and twenty yards. Game was nearly always shot while standing still, although an occasional rabbit was sho running. Arrows striking these small animals frequently passed com pletely through them. Death did not always result from the firs shot, and one or more additional arrows were sometimes necessary to kill.

If a rabbit were shot and caught, Ishi would break all its legs with his hands, then lay it on the ground to die from the shock. This seems to have been a hunting custom, and he seemed to dislike having the animal die in his hands. Later, he adopted, with us, the more humane method of tapping his game on the head to kill it.

Animals shot at do not always become alarmed, should the arrow miss them, but often permit several shots to be made. Quail struck with an arrow in fleshy parts, sometimes fly, or attempt to fly, with the missile transfixing them, and are only detained by its catching in the brush or foliage of trees.

In hunting deer, Ishi was particularly careful in the observance of several essential precautions. He would eat no fish on the day prior to the hunt, because the odor could be detected by deer, he said; nor would he have the odor of tobacco smoke about him. The morning of the hunt Ishi bathed himself from head to foot, and washed his mouth. Eating no food, he dressed himself in a shirt, or breech clout. Any covering on the legs made a noise while in the brush, and a sensitive skin rather favored cautious walking. While Ishi was proud of his shoes acquired in civilization, he said they made a noise like a horse, and he immediately discarded them when any real work in the field was encountered. In climbing cliffs, or crossing streams or trunks of trees, he first removed his shoes. So in hunting he preferred to go barefoot, and the strength of his perfectly shaped feet gave him a very definite advantage over his civilized companions.

It was a custom among his people to practice venesection before hunting expeditions. From Ishi's description, it appeared that this consisted of simple scarification over the flexor sides of the forearm and calf of the leg. This was supposed to strengthen and increase the courage of the hunter. Small chips of obsidian were used in this process.

In hunting deer, Ishi used the method of ambush. It was customary in his tribe to station archers behind certain rocks or bushes near well known deer trails. Then a band of Indians beat the brush at a mile or so distant, driving toward those in hiding. Upon our trip into Tehama County with Ishi, he showed us old deer trails near which curious small piles of rock were located at intervals hardly exceeding ten yards. These he indicated as ancient spots of ambush. They were just large enough to shield a man in a crouching position. The moss and lichen on them spoke of considerable age. One would hardly notice them in a boulder country, but the evidence of crude masonry was apparent when one's attention was called to them.

In approaching game, Ishi would rather skirt an entire mountain than come up on the wind side. His observance of this rule was almost an obsession. He tested the wind by wetting his little finger. In travel over the country, certain places would appeal to him as ground favorable for rabbits, quail, squirrel, wildcats, or bear.

His hut in Deer Creek cañon was built on an old bear trail, many of these animals having been trapped within a few miles by an old hermit-like trapper of those parts. Years ago this same man caught an old Indian in his bear trap, maiming him for life. Ishi admitted that this Indian was his relative, perhaps his uncle or stepfather.

When in a part of the country suitable for rabbits, Ishi would hide himself behind a bush and give the rabbit call. This consists of a kissing sound, made by the lips with two fingers pressed against them. It is a shrill, plaintive squeak or cry, identical with that made by a rabbit in distress. He repeated it often, and with heart-rending pathos. He said that jackrabbits, wildcats, coyotes, and bear would come to the call. The first came to protect its young; the others came expecting food. Upon one afternoon's hunt, to test the truth of his assertions, I had Ishi repeat this call twelve times. From these dozen calls came five rabbits, and one wildcat emerged from the brush and approached us. Some rabbits came from a distance of one hundred and fifty yards, and approached within ten yards. The wildcat came within fifty yards, and permitted me to discharge five arrows at him before a glancing hit sent him into the forest.

As the game drew near, Ishi kept up a sucking sort of kiss with his lips while he adjusted an arrow on the bow. When the game was within a dozen yards, he shot.

He also used a call for deer, which he said was effective only when the does were with fawns. He took a new, tender leaf of a madrone tree, folded it lengthwise, and placing it between his lips, sucked vigorously. The sound produced was somewhat similar to that made when a small boy blows on a blade of grass held between his thumbs. It resembles the plaintive bleat of a fawn.

In decoying deer, Ishi also used a deer's head. He had one in his original camp from which the horns had been removed, and it was stuffed with leaves and twigs. This he placed on his head, and raising it above a bush, attracted the attention of his game, stimulating its curiosity while luring it within bow shot.

In none of our trips with Ishi were we able to kill a deer. Upon several occasions we secured shots, but owing to the distance, fall of the ground, or lack of accuracy, we failed to hit. The nearest shot was at sixty yards, and this is well beyond the Indian range of effectiveness. That it is possible, however, to kill large game with the bow, we proved upon a subsequent hunting expedition with Mr. W. J. Compton. We shot and killed two deer with the English long bow. One of these bucks Mr. Compton shot running at 65 yards. The steel pointed arrow penetrated the chest and protruded a foot the other side, breaking off as the deer bounded through the brush. This animal died after running about 200 yards. I shot another buck at 45 yards. The arrow, penetrating just back of the diaphragm, caused an intense intra-abdominal hemorrhage, and death resulted after this deer had run a quarter of a mile. This would indicate that the Indians would have had little difficulty in striking down game. The arrows used by us were of the type of the old English broad head, 29 inches long, weighing from one ounce to an ounce and a half, heavily feathered.

and having steel heads one and one-half inches long by one inch wide.
Mr. Compton shot a six-foot yew bow weighing 65 pounds, while mine
was a sinew-backed yew bow 5 feet, 10 inches long, weighing 54 pounds.

In one deer killed with a rifle, I tested the penetrating power of
Ishi's arrows. Stationed at thirty yards, he drove one arrow through
the neck, half the shaft entering; the second shot struck the spine and
probably would have caused paralysis; the third arrow entered the
thorax back of the scapula, its head piercing the opposite chest wall.
This also would have been fatal.[7]

In shots at buzzards, hawks, and gulls in flight, it often occurred
that an arrow coming very close was dodged by these birds. To make
this less possible, Ishi smeared his arrow shaft with black mud, and
selected one with a close-cropped feather, that it might be less con-
spicuous and more silent than usual.

Our bad luck in deer hunting Ishi ascribed to the fact that I had
killed a rattlesnake on the trail. He respected these reptiles, and
always preferred to walk around a snake, wishing him well and leaving
him unharmed.

Besides using the ambush, Ishi waited at deer licks to secure his
venison. He had no special care for female deer, but considered them
all good meat. He also shot fawns if needed for food. Those were the
days of abundance of game, and the Indian killed only for food.

He preserved his deer meat by a process of curing in smoke, just
as all hunters today make jerky. The deer hide he or more likely his
female relatives, prepared by first rubbing in the brains and later by
drying and scraping. Ishi himself did not seem to know how to make
a fine quality of buckskin. His needlework and moccasin making were
also not of an advanced type. In the University Museum we have a
fur robe, previously the property of Ishi. It is composed of many wildcat and raccoon skins sewn together. Here the preparation is of a very
good type. The furs are soft, fairly smooth and seem to have been
smoked. This process of smoking, common among Indians, saturates
the hide with creosote compounds, thus preserving the tissue from
bacteria and parasites, while it renders it soft and somewhat water-
proof. The absence of wounds in these skins suggests that Ishi used a
trap or snare rather than the bow, to secure the pelts.

Ishi told us many times the methods he and his people used in
killing bear. It was their ancient custom for a number of men to
surround an animal, building a circle of fire about him. They then dis-

[7] There are interesting facts on the penetrating power of the arrow in Thomas
Wilson's Arrow Wounds, *in* the American Anthropologist, n. s., III, 513–600, 1901.

charged arrows at him, attempting to shoot him in the mouth, and preferring to use rather small obsidian points, thinking that these made a more severe wound. If the animal charged an Indian, he defended himself with a fire brand, while the other members of the partly shot the bear with arrows. The shooting distance seems to have been twenty yards or less. The whole process seems to have been one of baiting and slowly wearing down the animal by hemorrhage and fatigue.

Among the specimens obtained by the University Museum is a skin of a cinnamon bear, which was shot by Ishi perhaps twenty-five years ago. It presents two cuts that indicate arrow and knife wounds. Ishi said that he killed this by shooting it with an arrow in the heart region, and later dispatching it with a short spear or obsidian knife. Owing to our imperfect language communication, and Ishi's natural modesty, we were unable to get minute details of this feat, but apparently the Indian killed the beast single-handed.

Shooting fish with the bow does not seem to have been one of his occupations. He used a salmon spear most expertly, and he also poisoned fish by putting the beaten fruit of squirting cucumber in trout pools. Fishhooks he made of bone, and wicker weirs were constructed for trout; but these things, of course, are not a part of archery.

Poisoned arrows he never used, although he knew of a method of making poison. This was to induce a rattlesnake to discharge its venom into a piece of deer liver, when, after putrefaction, the arrowheads were smeared with this combined bacterial poison and venom.

Ishi could imitate the call of many birds and small animals, and his name for these creatures had a remarkable phonetic resemblance to their call. Mountain quail he named *tsakaka;* the wild goose was *wami;* the gray squirrel, *dadichu.* These lower animals he believed fellow creatures, and all had acted human parts at times. The lizards, because of their hands, once made bows and arrows. Their bobbing motion, when on a sunny rock, was work of some sort. The yellow tendrils of the love vine or dodder were made by them at night to snare deer. The barking squirrel in the treetop told him of a near-by fox or wildcat. A story was built around every animal, and these mythical ideas he believed must be taken into consideration when hunting.

Various places had odors suggestive of certain animals. Ishi said that white men smelled bad, like a horse.

To have a bow break in the hand while shooting, Ishi considered a very serious omen and a portent of sickness. Thus he accounted for an attack of paratyphoid fever which one of us contracted. He himself had two bows shatter in his grasp, and doubtless this and several other malign influences incident to our civilization, in his mind, contributed as causes of his own last illness. During the declining days of his life, the one thing that brought that happy smile to his face which characterized him, was the subject of archery. A little work, feathering arrows or binding points on with sinew, gave him more pleasure than any diversion we could offer. Even when too weak to work, he liked to show me some little trick or method in making a shaft or backing a bow. To the last his heart was in the game. When he died and was cremated according to the custom of his people, we placed by his side some tobacco, ten pieces of dentalium shell, a little acorn meal, a bit of jerky, his fire sticks, a quiver full of arrows, and his bow.

EXPLANATION OF PLATES

PLATE 22

Death mask of Ishi who died of pulmonary tuberculosis, March 25, 1916.

DEATH MASK OF ISHI

PLATE 23

Fig. 1.—Hickory bow, backed with glued catgut. Made in 1914. A stron[g] shooting bow, often used by Ishi. University of California Museum of Anthro[po]pology, specimen number 1–19867.

Fig. 2.—Unbacked ash bow, broken in use. It is much longer than Ish[i] usually made, 54 inches. Museum number 1–19451.

Fig. 3.—A yew bow, made on the normal proportions, backed with dee[r] tendon. This specimen was broken in testing, before application of the backing[.] Museum number 1–19452.

Fig. 4.—Oregon yew bow, backed with thin rawhide. This was one o[f] Ishi's best bows, used most at targets. Museum number 1–19590. Length, 4[9] inches. The hand grip, on all the above specimens, is woolen tape.

Fig. 5.—Quiver of otter skin. Specimen number 1–19566. The containe[d] bow and arrows were made by Ishi at the Museum. The quiver is an origina[l] piece, taken when the camp of his people was discovered in 1908.

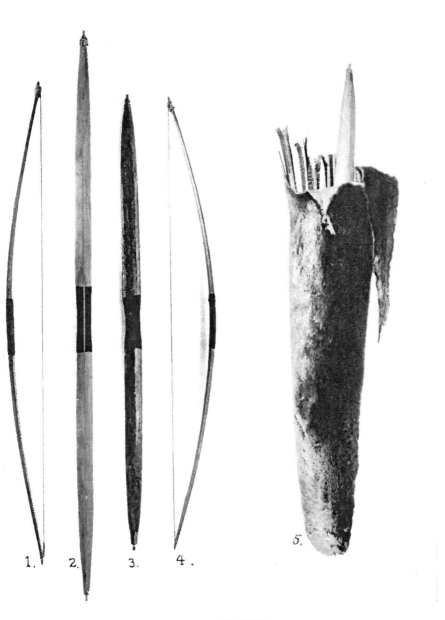

YAHI BOWS AND QUIVER

PLATE 24

Figures 1 to 3 are old Yahi arrows; 4 to 9, specimens made while Ishi was at the Museum.

Fig. 1.—Shaft of hazel, foreshaft of some heavier wood, possibly dogwood There is a notch for a head, but this is missing. Buzzard wing feathers Length, 29⅜ inches, weight 320 grains. University of California Museum of Anthropology, number 1-19577.

Fig. 2.—The same type as above, feathers a trifle longer. Both are painted with alternate red and blue rings and intervening wavy lines. Museum number 1-19578.

Fig. 3.—The shaft is like the preceding, but the point is here preserved It is a small serrated head of window glass. There is blood on the arrow Museum number 1-19579.

Fig. 4.—A one-piece hazel shaft, feathered with turkey feathers, pointed with an obsidian head. Commercial pigments and shellac embellish this arrow Number 1-19864.

Fig. 5.—This is the type of arrow Ishi adopted after living in civilizatio It is made of a ⁵⁄₁₆ birch dowel, gayly painted, feathered with blue heron feathers and is tipped with a steel head, sinew bound. Number 1-19863.

Fig. 6.—This is a dowel—turkey tail feathers, blue and red paint ring obsidian head. An arrow made for show. Number 1-19866.

Fig. 7.—A longer type of service arrow of Japanese bamboo with sho birch foreshaft and steel head. Used in early target practice and huntin Number 1-19862.

Fig. 8.—A blunt-pointed arrow of native bamboo, buckeye foreshaft, ga colors, turkey tail feathers. Made for exhibition or gift. Number 1-19456.

Fig. 9.—Same as last, only it has an obsidian head. Length 38 inches, weigh 580 grains. Number 1-19454. Similar shafts Ishi made and gave to Secretar Lane at a ceremonial occasion in San Francisco in 1914.

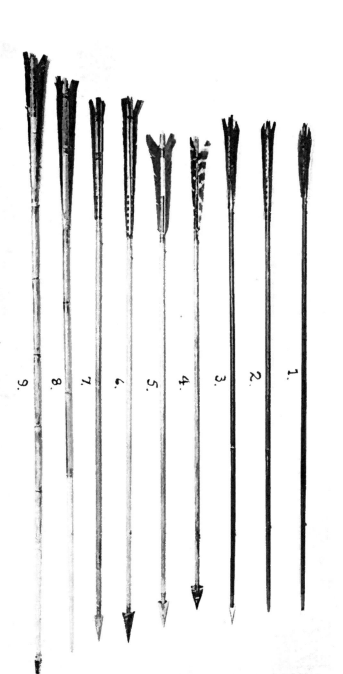

PLATE 25

Fig. 1.—Chewing sinew for arrow wrapping.

Fig. 2.—Heating resin to be used on end of a shaft to affix the head on the arrow.

Fig. 3.—Sinew being applied to the arrowhead and shaft.

Fig. 1.

Fig. 2.

Fig. 3.

PLATE 27

Fig. 1.—Aboriginal bone-pointed arrowflaker. This is from the Y tribe in northwestern California and illustrates the type used by the Yahi be iron was known. Length, 17⅜ inches. University of California Museum Anthropology, specimen number 1–2496.

Fig. 2.—Iron flaker made and used by Ishi while in captivity. Num 1–19591.

Fig. 3.—Flaker for fine retouching.

Fig. 4.—Leather pad to cover the ball of the hand in flaking.

Fig. 5.—Bone struck a glancing blow in order to detach pieces from a of obsidian.

Fig. 6.—Stone used as a mallet to strike bone.

Fig. 7.—Obsidian struck from a larger mass.

Fig. 8.—Flake as detached previous to the retouching process.

Fig. 9.—Obsidian arrow point taking shape.

Fig. 10.—Obsidian arrow nearing completion.

Fig. 11.—Completed obsidian arrow point.

Fig. 12.—Minute flakes and chips detached in the retouching.

Fig. 13.—A small, broad arrow point of obsidian. Length, 1 inch; w 11/16 inch; thickness, ⅛ inch; weight, 15 grains.

Fig. 14.—Long, narrow arrowhead made of plate glass. Ishi made n such show pieces. They are too long and fragile for use.

Fig. 15.—Obsidian arrowhead. Length, 2 inches; width 15/16 inch; thick ¼ inch; weight, 60 grains.

Fig. 16.—Glass arrowhead, made from a blue medicine bottle.

Fig. 17.—A glass arrowhead, made from a brown beer bottle. Length inches; width, 1 inch; thickness 3/16 inch; weight 90 grains.

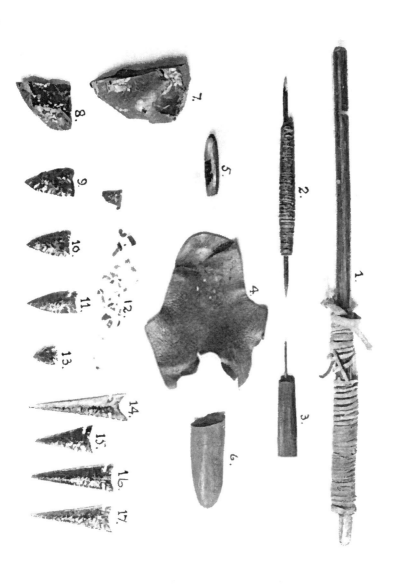

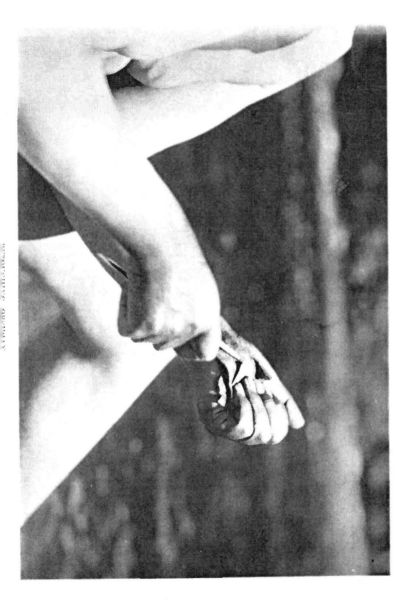

STANDING SHOT

KNEELING SHOT

PLATE 32

Fig. 1.—Chopping a stick of juniper into rough shape for a bow.

Fig. 2.—A shot from a squatting position, a characteristic attitude in Ishi's archery.

Fig. 3.—Calling game.

Fig. 1.   Fig. 3.

Fig. 2.

BOW MAKING AND HUNTING

PLATE 33

Fig. 1.—Watching the flight of the arrow. The bow string is still vibrating. The bow has turned in Ishi's grasp in a manner that was habitual with him. He holds an extra arrow in his right armpit.

Fig. 2.—Carrying the bow and arrow. This is a 54-inch hunting bow of cedar, pulling 45 pounds. The arrows are steel-pointed.

PLATE 34

An original specimen taken from the camp which the Yahi were inhabiting in 1908. It now forms number 1-19564 in the Anthropological Museum of the University.

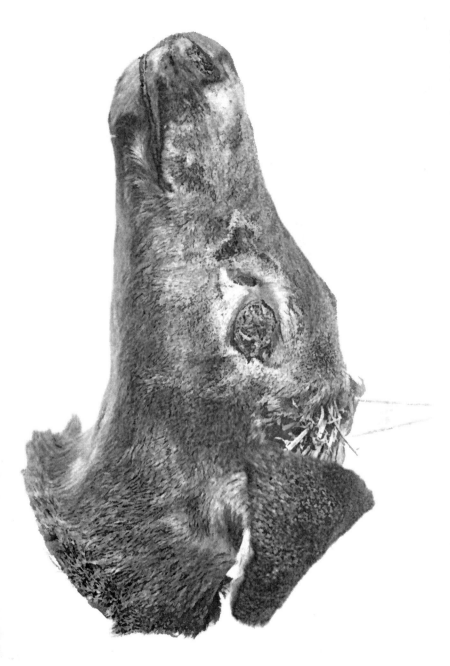

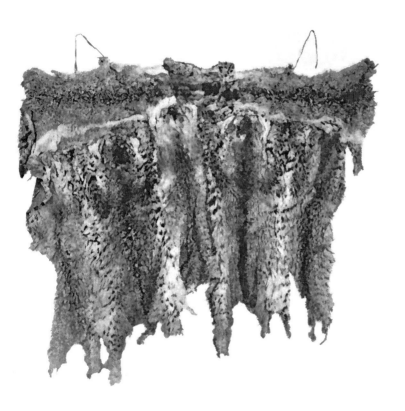

CAPE OF WILDCAT SKINS

PLATE 36

From a cinematograph film

Fig. 1.——Nocking an arrow on the string.

Fig. 2.——Full drawn, wrist touching the chin.

Fig. 1

PREPARING TO SHOOT

Fig. 2

Fig. 1

AFTER THE RELEASE   Fig. 2

Printed in the United States
114817LV00002B/125/A